636.68
GRA

D1162168

DATE DUE

DOLTON PUBLIC LIBRARY DISTRICT
708 849-2385

¡Las mascotas son geniales!
Pets Are Awesome!

MI PÁJARO

MY BIRD

Norman D. Graubart
Traducción al español: Christina Green

PowerKiDS press.

New York

3659434
Dolton Public Library District

Published in 2014 by The Rosen Publishing Group, Inc.
29 East 21st Street, New York, NY 10010

Copyright © 2014 by The Rosen Publishing Group, Inc.

All rights reserved. No part of this book may be reproduced in any form without permission in writing from the publisher, except by a reviewer.

First Edition

Book Design: Colleen Bialecki
Photo Research: Katie Stryker

Traducción al español: Christina Green

Photo Credits: Cover chloe7992/Shutterstock.com; p. 5 Edoma/Shutterstock.com; p. 7 Victor Soares/Shutterstock.com; p. 9 Natalia D./Shutterstock.com; p. 11 Eduardo Rivero/Shutterstock.com; p. 13 44kmos/Shutterstock.com; p. 15 Donjiy/Shutterstock.com; p. 17 nadi555/Shutterstock.com; p. 19 Dima Fadeev/Shutterstock.com; p. 21 Vishnevskiy Vasily/Shutterstock.com; p 23 Eric Cote/Shutterstock.com.

Library of Congress Cataloging-in-Publication Data

Graubart, Norman D.
My bird = Mi pájaro / by Norman D. Graubart ; translated by Christina Green. – First edition.
    pages cm. – (Pets are awesome! = ¡Las mascotas son geniales!)
English and Spanish.
Includes index.
ISBN 978-1-4777-3310-3 (library)
1. Birds–Juvenile literature. 2. Cage birds–Juvenile literature. I. Green, Christina, translator. II. Graubart, Norman D. My bird. III. Graubart, Norman D. My bird. Spanish. IV. Title. V. Title: Mi pájaro.
QL676.2.G71818 2014
636.6'8–dc23

2013022580

Web Sites: Due to the changing nature of Internet links, PowerKids Press has developed an online list of websites related to the subject of this book. This site is updated regularly. Please use this link to access the list: www.powerkidslinks.com/paa/bird/

Manufactured in the United States of America

CPSIA Compliance Information: Batch # W14PK3: For Further Information contact Rosen Publishing, New York, New York at 1-800-237-9932

CONTENIDO

CONTENTS

Hay muchas clases de pájaros.
Muchos de ellos pueden ser mascotas.

There are many kinds of birds. Many types can be kept as pets.

4

Las cacatúas son **pájaros con cresta**. Esto significa que tienen un penacho de **plumas** en la cabeza.

Cockatoos are **crested birds**. This means they have **feathers** that stick up on their heads.

7

El pájaro más común como mascota es el **periquito**.

The most common pet bird is the **parakeet**.

9

Los pájaros, o en general las aves, son los únicos animales con plumas.
Las plumas les permiten volar.

Birds are the only animals with feathers. Feathers make flight possible.

Los colibríes zunzuncito son los pájaros más pequeños.

Bee hummingbirds are the smallest birds.

Las cacatúas ninfas, o carolinas, se alimentan principalmente de semillas. Todas las carolinas silvestres vienen de Australia.

Cockatiels eat mostly seeds. All wild cockatiels come from Australia.

Los avestruces son aves que no vuelan. Son las aves más grandes del mundo.

Ostriches are flightless birds. They are the largest birds in the world.

Algunos pájaros mascota pueden vivir por mucho tiempo. Las guacamayas pueden vivir más de 70 años.

Some pet birds can live for a very long time. Scarlet macaws can live to be more than 70 years old.

Este gorrión doméstico come un insecto. Muchos pájaros comen insectos.

This house sparrow is eating a bug. Many birds eat bugs.

20

21

Si eres amable con tu pájaro mascota, él será amable contigo.

———————————————

If you are gentle with your pet bird, it will be gentle with you.

PALABRAS QUE DEBES SABER
WORDS TO KNOW

(el) pájaro con
cresta
crested bird

(las) plumas
feathers

(los) periquitos
parakeets

ÍNDICE

INDEX